THE LAW OF ABUNDANCE

How to Attract Wealth and Abundance into Your Life

Victor Solano

INTRODUCTION

Welcome to The Law of Abundance, a book that will transform your life by helping you unlock the secrets to attracting wealth and success. This book is designed to provide you with practical tools and techniques that will enable you to cultivate an abundance mindset, attract prosperity, and live a life of fulfillment and purpose.

Abundance is more than just having an abundance of money. It encompasses all aspects of life, including health, relationships, opportunities, and more. Abundance is about having a mindset that attracts and creates wealth and prosperity in every area of life. When you have an abundance mindset, you can create a life filled with joy, purpose, and abundance.

Importance of Mindset in Attracting Wealth and Success

Your mindset is a critical factor in attracting wealth and success.

If you have a negative mindset, it will be difficult to attract abundance and prosperity into your life. Your thoughts and beliefs create your reality, so it's essential to have a positive mindset that aligns with your desires.

Having a positive mindset is about believing in yourself, trusting the universe, and having faith that you can achieve anything you set your mind to. When you have a positive mindset, you will attract positive experiences and opportunities into your life. Conversely, if you have a negative mindset, you will attract negative experiences and struggle to achieve your goals.

How This Book Will Help You Unlock the Secrets to Abundance

This book will help you develop an abundance mindset, attract wealth and success, and live a life of purpose and fulfillment. The Law of Abundance is a comprehensive guide that covers a range of topics, including understanding abundance, the power of belief, visualization and affirmations, gratitude and the law of attraction, setting goals for abundance, the art of giving and receiving, building wealth through passive income, investing in yourself, networking, cultivating an abundance mindset, overcoming fear, money management, relationships, harnessing the power of intuition, spirituality, the impact of environment on wealth, time management and productivity, embracing change, and the power of positive thinking.

By reading this book, you will learn how to identify and overcome limiting beliefs, develop empowering beliefs, craft powerful affirmations, practice gratitude, set SMART goals, create passive income streams, invest in your personal development, build a strong network, develop an abundance mindset, overcome fear, manage your money, attract abundant relationships, harness the power of intuition, practice mindfulness and meditation, create an environment that fosters success, increase productivity, embrace change and adaptability, and cultivate a positive mindset.

You will also learn about the law of attraction and how it can help you manifest your desires, the importance of generosity and giving, the impact of your environment on your mindset, and the power of positive thinking. You will discover how to create a personalized plan for wealth attraction and maintain momentum and accountability.

The Law of Abundance is a book that will change your life. By following the guidance provided in this book, you will unlock the secrets to abundance and attract wealth and success into your life. You will learn how to cultivate an abundance mindset, set and achieve goals, build wealth through passive income, invest in yourself, network effectively, harness the power of intuition, practice mindfulness and meditation, manage your money, cultivate positive relationships, and embrace change and adaptability.

The Law of Abundance is a transformative guide that will help you create the life of your dreams. By committing to personal growth and applying the principles shared in this book, you can achieve greater levels of success, wealth, and fulfillment. So, let's begin this incredible journey together, and I encourage you to share your experiences and insights with others. Together, we can create a community of like-minded individuals who are committed to living an abundant life. As we move forward through each chapter, remember that you are not alone on this journey. You have the power to transform your life and unlock the secrets to abundance.

UNDERSTANDING ABUNDANCE

Chapter 1

If you're looking to attract wealth and abundance into your life, the first step is to understand what abundance truly means. Many people associate abundance with material possessions or financial wealth, but in reality, it's much more than that. Abundance encompasses all aspects of life, including health, happiness, love, and fulfillment.

Defining Abundance and Wealth

Abundance can be defined as having an ample supply or more than enough of something. This can apply to material possessions, but it also includes intangible assets such as health, happiness, and personal fulfillment. Wealth, on the other hand, is often associated with financial prosperity, but it can also refer to the abundance of resources, opportunities, and relationships in

VICTOR SOLANO

your life.

Debunking Common Misconceptions

One of the most common misconceptions about abundance is that it's only attainable for a select few. Many people believe that abundance is reserved for the wealthy or privileged, but this couldn't be further from the truth. Abundance is available to everyone, regardless of their financial status, background, or circumstances.

Another misconception is that abundance is solely determined by external factors, such as luck or fate. While external circumstances can certainly play a role in one's life, the most important factor in attracting abundance is your mindset and belief system.

The Role of Mindset in Attracting Abundance

Your mindset and belief system are crucial components in attracting abundance into your life. Your thoughts and beliefs create a vibrational frequency that attracts experiences and opportunities that align with your energy. If you have a positive and abundant mindset, you will naturally attract abundance into your life. However, if you have a scarcity mindset, you'll likely attract lack and limitation.

Your mindset is shaped by your beliefs, which are often developed early in life and influenced by your environment, culture, and experiences. Many of these beliefs are limiting and can hold you back from experiencing abundance. For example, you may have been told that money is the root of all evil, or that you have to work hard to make a living. These beliefs can create a subconscious block that prevents you from experiencing abundance.

To attract abundance, you must identify and release limiting beliefs and replace them with empowering ones. This requires a shift in your mindset and a commitment to personal growth and development.

In summary, understanding the true meaning of abundance and

wealth is essential in attracting them into your life. By debunking common misconceptions and recognizing the role of mindset in attracting abundance, you can begin to shift your beliefs and create a more abundant life. In the next chapter, we'll explore the power of belief and how it shapes your reality.

THE POWER OF BELIEF

Chapter 2

Beliefs are the driving force behind our thoughts, emotions, and actions. They are deeply ingrained within us and shape our perception of reality. Our beliefs determine the opportunities we see, the choices we make, and ultimately, the outcomes we experience. In this chapter, we will explore the significance of beliefs in shaping reality, how to identify and overcome limiting beliefs, and techniques to develop empowering beliefs that will help attract wealth and abundance into your life.

The Significance of Beliefs in Shaping Reality

Our beliefs act as filters through which we view the world. They are formed based on our experiences, upbringing, cultural background, and education. Our beliefs about ourselves, others, and the world around us are powerful enough to shape our reality.

When we believe that we are capable of achieving our goals, we are more likely to take action towards achieving them. Conversely, when we hold limiting beliefs about our abilities, we create self-imposed limitations that prevent us from reaching our full potential.

Identifying and Overcoming Limiting Beliefs

Limiting beliefs are those that hold us back from reaching our full potential. They are often negative and irrational, and they prevent us from taking action towards achieving our goals. Common limiting beliefs include "I'm not good enough," "I don't deserve success," or "I'm too old/young to achieve my dreams."

To identify your limiting beliefs, you need to pay attention to your self-talk. Notice the negative thoughts that come up when you think about your goals or your abilities. Write them down and examine them objectively. Ask yourself, "Is this belief true? Is there evidence to support it?" Challenge your limiting beliefs by finding evidence that contradicts them. For example, if you believe that you're not good enough to start your own business, remind yourself of times when you have succeeded in the past.

Techniques to Develop Empowering Beliefs

Once you have identified your limiting beliefs, you can start developing empowering beliefs that will help you attract wealth and abundance into your life. Empowering beliefs are positive, realistic, and aligned with your goals and values.

Here are some techniques to help you develop empowering beliefs:

1. **Reframe your negative self-talk**: Instead of saying "I'm not good enough," say "I'm capable of learning and growing." This reframing helps you focus on your potential rather than your limitations.

2. **Visualize success**: Visualize yourself achieving your goals and experiencing abundance in your life. This visualization helps you align your thoughts and beliefs with your desired outcomes.

3. **Use positive affirmations**: Affirmations are positive

statements that you repeat to yourself to reinforce empowering beliefs. For example, "I am worthy of success and abundance" or "I am capable of achieving my goals."

4. **Surround yourself with positivity**: Surround yourself with people who support and encourage your goals. Read positive books, listen to uplifting music, and watch inspiring movies. This helps you maintain a positive mindset and reinforces your empowering beliefs.

5. **Take action**: Take small steps towards your goals, even if they are outside your comfort zone. The more you take action towards your goals, the more you will believe in your ability to achieve them.

In conclusion, our beliefs are powerful enough to shape our reality. By identifying and overcoming limiting beliefs and developing empowering beliefs, we can attract wealth and abundance into our lives. Reframe your negative self-talk, visualize success, use positive affirmations, surround yourself with positivity, and take action towards your goals. These techniques will help you develop an abundance mindset that aligns your thoughts and beliefs with your desired outcomes. Remember, you are capable of achieving your goals and experiencing abundance in your life. Believe in yourself, and you will attract the wealth and abundance that you deserve.

VISUALIZATION AND AFFIRMATIONS

Chapter 3

Have you ever heard of the phrase, "seeing is believing"? Visualization is the act of creating vivid mental images of your desired outcome or goal. It is a powerful tool that can help you attract wealth and abundance into your life. Visualization can help you to align your thoughts, beliefs, and emotions with the reality that you want to create.

The Science Behind Visualization

Visualization is not just a fanciful idea; there is actual science behind it. When you visualize, you activate the same neural networks in your brain that are activated when you perform a physical action. For example, when you visualize yourself playing tennis, the same areas of your brain that are active when you play tennis are also active when you visualize it.

In fact, studies have shown that athletes who use visualization techniques improve their performance and increase their chances of success. Visualization also helps to reduce anxiety and stress, which can be detrimental to your overall well-being and hinder your ability to attract abundance.

Crafting Powerful Affirmations

Affirmations are positive statements that you repeat to yourself daily to help reprogram your subconscious mind. They are a powerful tool to help you create a more positive and abundant mindset. When you repeat affirmations, you send a message to your subconscious mind that you believe in yourself, your abilities, and your worthiness to receive abundance.

Crafting powerful affirmations involves choosing words and phrases that align with your desired outcome or goal. Affirmations should be in the present tense, and they should be stated in a positive way. For example, "I am abundant" is a more powerful affirmation than "I am not broke."

It's also essential to make your affirmations personal and specific. Use words that resonate with you and align with your values. For example, if you value creativity, your affirmation could be "I am a creative genius who attracts abundant opportunities."

Daily Practices for Success

Visualization and affirmations are powerful tools for attracting abundance, but like anything else, consistency is key. Daily practice is essential to reprogram your subconscious mind and shift your mindset toward abundance.

Here are a few daily practices to help you attract wealth and abundance into your life:

1. **Morning Visualization and Affirmations**: Start your day by visualizing your desired outcome or goal. Create a vivid mental image of what it looks like and feels like to achieve that goal. Then, repeat your affirmations to yourself, focusing on your desired outcome.

2. **Gratitude Journaling**: Take a few minutes each day to write down things you are grateful for. Focusing on gratitude helps to shift your mindset toward abundance and attracts more things to be grateful for.

3. **Mid-Day Visualization**: Take a few minutes during your lunch break to visualize your desired outcome or goal. This can help you stay focused and motivated throughout the day.

4. **Evening Visualization and Affirmations**: End your day by visualizing your desired outcome or goal once again. Then, repeat your affirmations, focusing on your desired outcome.

Remember, the Law of Abundance is about attracting wealth and abundance into your life. Visualization and affirmations are powerful tools that can help you achieve your goals and attract the abundance that you deserve. By practicing these techniques consistently, you can shift your mindset toward abundance and create the life that you desire.

GRATITUDE AND THE LAW OF ATTRACTION

Chapter 4

Gratitude is an essential component of attracting abundance into our lives. When we focus on the good things we already have, we send a positive message to the universe that we are open to receiving more of the same. This chapter will explore the importance of gratitude in attracting abundance, how it rewires the brain, and practical exercises that can help us cultivate a spirit of gratitude.

The Importance of Gratitude in Attracting Abundance

Gratitude is a powerful tool for attracting abundance. When we are grateful for what we have, we send out a positive vibration to the universe, and we attract more positive experiences into our lives. Gratitude helps us focus on the good things in our lives, rather than what is lacking. When we focus on the positive, we attract more positivity, and this leads to greater abundance.

Gratitude also helps us to shift our focus from what we lack to what we have. Often, we can get so caught up in our desire for more that we forget to appreciate what we already have. By cultivating a spirit of gratitude, we learn to appreciate the present moment and the abundance that already exists in our lives.

How Gratitude Rewires the Brain

Gratitude has a transformative effect on our brains. When we express gratitude, our brains release dopamine and serotonin, which are neurotransmitters that make us feel good. These chemicals not only make us feel good in the moment, but they also create a positive feedback loop in our brains. The more we express gratitude, the more our brains release dopamine and serotonin, and the more positive we feel. This positive feedback loop helps to rewire our brains, making us more inclined to focus on the positive aspects of our lives.

Practical Gratitude Exercises

Gratitude is a practice that can be cultivated through various exercises.

Here are a few practical gratitude exercises that can help you develop a more grateful mindset:

1. **Gratitude Journal**: Start a gratitude journal where you write down three things that you are grateful for every day. This exercise helps you focus on the positive things in your life, and it also helps you cultivate a more positive mindset.

2. **Gratitude Walk**: Take a walk in nature and focus on the things that you are grateful for. This exercise helps you connect with nature and appreciate the beauty that surrounds you.

3. **Gratitude Meditation**: Practice a gratitude meditation where you focus on the things that you are grateful for. This exercise helps you cultivate a deeper sense of gratitude and

can also help you reduce stress and anxiety.

4. **Gratitude Letters**: Write a letter to someone expressing your gratitude for them. This exercise not only helps you cultivate a sense of gratitude, but it also strengthens your relationships with others.

Gratitude is an essential component of attracting abundance into our lives. By focusing on the positive aspects of our lives and cultivating a spirit of gratitude, we send a positive message to the universe that we are open to receiving more of the same. Gratitude also has a transformative effect on our brains, rewiring them to focus on the positive aspects of our lives. By practicing gratitude exercises such as journaling, walking in nature, meditating, and writing gratitude letters, we can cultivate a more grateful mindset and attract more abundance into our lives. Remember, the more we express gratitude, the more positive experiences we attract into our lives.

SETTING GOALS FOR ABUNDANCE

Chapter 5

Setting goals is a crucial step in the journey towards abundance. Without clear and specific goals, it's difficult to know where you're headed, and you're less likely to achieve the success and prosperity you desire. In this chapter, we'll explore how to set SMART goals, align them with your values, and take action towards achieving abundance.

Creating SMART Goals

The first step in setting effective goals is to ensure they are SMART. SMART is an acronym for Specific, Measurable, Achievable, Relevant, and Time-bound. Specific goals are clear and unambiguous, stating exactly what you want to achieve. Measurable goals are quantifiable, allowing you to track your progress and determine when you've reached your objective.

Achievable goals are realistic and feasible, taking into account your current abilities and resources. Relevant goals are aligned with your values and larger life purpose, providing meaning and motivation. Time-bound goals have a specific deadline or timeframe, providing a sense of urgency and focus.

For example, a goal like "I want to make more money" is not specific, measurable, achievable, or time-bound. It's also not necessarily relevant to your values or larger life purpose. Instead, a SMART goal might be "I want to increase my monthly income by 20% over the next six months by securing a higher-paying job or launching a profitable side business."

Aligning Goals with Your Values

It's essential to align your goals with your values and larger life purpose. When your goals are congruent with what matters most to you, you'll feel more motivated, energized, and fulfilled. Start by identifying your core values, such as family, health, creativity, community, spirituality, or personal growth. Then, consider how your goals align with these values. Are they helping you to live a more meaningful and fulfilling life? Are they supporting your long-term vision and purpose?

For instance, if one of your core values is community, a relevant goal might be to volunteer at a local charity or start a community-building project. If personal growth is essential to you, a relevant goal might be to enroll in a course or attend a workshop that aligns with your interests and goals.

The Role of Action in Achieving Abundance

Setting SMART goals that align with your values is only the first step towards abundance. To achieve success and prosperity, you must take action towards your goals consistently. Action is what turns your dreams into reality, allowing you to overcome obstacles, learn from failures, and make progress towards your desired outcomes.

Start by breaking down your goals into smaller, actionable steps. This makes them more manageable and less overwhelming, allowing you to focus on making progress one step at a time. For example, if your goal is to increase your income by 20% over the next six months, your actionable steps might include updating your resume, researching higher-paying job opportunities, networking with professionals in your field, or launching a side business that aligns with your skills and interests.

It's also crucial to prioritize your actions, focusing on the most critical tasks that will have the greatest impact on your progress towards your goals. This requires discipline, focus, and time management skills, but it's essential for achieving abundance. Remember that consistent action, even in small amounts, can lead to significant progress over time.

Finally, it's vital to monitor your progress towards your goals regularly. This allows you to adjust your actions or strategies as needed, staying on track and motivated towards achieving abundance. Celebrate your successes along the way, no matter how small they may seem. Recognize the progress you've made and use it as fuel to keep moving forward towards even greater success and prosperity.

Setting goals that are SMART, aligned with your values, and backed by consistent action is the key to unlocking the power of abundance in your life. By following the principles outlined in this chapter, you'll be well on your way to achieving your goals and creating the life of abundance you desire.

Remember that setting goals is a continual process, and it's essential to review and adjust them regularly as circumstances change. By staying committed to your vision and taking consistent action towards your goals, you can create a life of abundance that aligns with your values and larger purpose.

In the next chapter, we'll explore the art of giving and receiving and how generosity can play a powerful role in attracting wealth and abundance into your life.

THE ART OF GIVING AND RECEIVING

Chapter 6

As you progress on your journey towards abundance, you will come to realize that giving and receiving are two sides of the same coin. To attract wealth and abundance into your life, you must cultivate an attitude of generosity and learn how to balance giving and receiving in all aspects of your life.

The Importance of Generosity in Attracting Wealth

Generosity is the act of giving freely and without expectation of reward. When you are generous, you create a positive energy that attracts more abundance into your life. This is because generosity creates a sense of abundance within you, which is then reflected in your external circumstances.

Generosity can take many forms, from donating money to charity to volunteering your time to help those in need. The important thing is to give freely and with an open heart, without expecting anything in return.

The Power of Reciprocity

The act of giving also creates a sense of reciprocity. When you give freely to others, you create a positive energy that is returned to you in the form of abundance. This is known as the law of reciprocity, which states that the universe will return to you what you give out.

However, it's important to note that giving should never be done with the expectation of receiving something in return. Instead, it should be done out of a genuine desire to help others and make a positive impact in the world.

Balancing Giving and Receiving in Life

While giving is important, it's equally important to balance this with receiving. Many people struggle with receiving because they feel guilty or unworthy of receiving abundance. This can create a blockage in the flow of abundance in your life.

To overcome this blockage, it's important to recognize that receiving is just as important as giving. When you receive abundance, you are able to create more abundance in your life and help others in the process.

To balance giving and receiving, you must first learn to receive with gratitude. This means acknowledging and appreciating the abundance that comes into your life, no matter how small it may seem. When you receive with gratitude, you create a positive energy that attracts more abundance into your life.

You must also learn to set healthy boundaries around giving and receiving. This means being aware of your own needs and limits, and not overextending yourself in the process of giving. It's important to give freely, but also to prioritize your own well-being and self-care.

Finally, it's important to recognize that giving and receiving are not mutually exclusive. When you give freely and with an open heart, you will naturally attract more abundance into your life. And when you receive with gratitude, you create a positive energy that allows you to give even more freely.

The art of giving and receiving is a vital component of attracting wealth and abundance into your life. By cultivating an attitude of generosity, you create a positive energy that attracts more abundance into your life. And by learning to balance giving and receiving, you create a flow of abundance that allows you to make a positive impact in the world.

Remember, giving and receiving are two sides of the same coin. When you give freely and receive with gratitude, you create a positive energy that allows you to attract even more abundance into your life. So be generous, be grateful, and allow the flow of abundance to guide you towards a life of prosperity and fulfillment.

BUILDING WEALTH THROUGH PASSIVE INCOME

Chapter 7

Passive income is a powerful tool that can help you achieve financial independence and create long-term wealth. Unlike active income, which requires you to trade time for money, passive income streams allow you to generate revenue without being actively involved in the process.

Understanding Passive Income Streams

Passive income is income that is earned without your active involvement. It typically comes from assets that you own, such as rental properties, stocks, bonds, or businesses. The key to generating passive income is to build assets that produce revenue consistently over time.

There are many different types of passive income streams, and each has its advantages and disadvantages.

Some common examples include:

- **Rental income**: This is income generated from renting out property that you own, such as an apartment or house. Rental income can provide a steady stream of cash flow, but it requires a significant upfront investment and ongoing maintenance and management.

- **Dividend income**: This is income earned from owning stocks that pay dividends. Dividend income can provide a reliable source of income, but it is subject to fluctuations in the stock market.

- **Interest income**: This is income earned from owning bonds or other fixed-income investments. Interest income can provide a predictable source of income, but it is subject to changes in interest rates.

• **Affiliate marketing**: This is income earned by promoting other people's products and earning a commission on sales. Affiliate marketing can be a low-risk way to generate passive income, but it requires a significant amount of time and effort to build an audience and establish credibility.

Strategies for Generating Passive Income

Building passive income streams takes time, effort, and patience. There are no shortcuts or get-rich-quick schemes that will help you achieve financial independence overnight. However, with a solid strategy and a long-term perspective, you can build a portfolio of assets that generate consistent passive income over time.

Here are some strategies for generating passive income:

• **Start small**: Don't try to build multiple passive income streams at once. Instead, start with one or two and focus on building them up over time. This will help you avoid spreading yourself too thin and ensure that you are giving each stream the attention it needs to be successful.

· **Choose the right asset**: Not all assets are created equal. When selecting an asset to invest in, consider factors such as potential return on investment, risk, and liquidity. Choose an asset that aligns with your financial goals and risk tolerance.

· **Diversify**: Don't put all your eggs in one basket. Diversify your portfolio by investing in multiple assets across different industries and asset classes. This will help mitigate risk and ensure that you have a steady stream of income even if one asset underperforms.

· **Be patient**: Building passive income streams takes time. Don't expect to see significant results overnight. Instead, focus on building a strong foundation and being consistent in your efforts. Over time, your passive income streams will grow and become more valuable.

· **Keep learning**: The world of passive income is constantly evolving. Stay up to date on the latest trends, strategies, and technologies to ensure that you are making informed decisions and maximizing your returns.

Managing Risks and Diversification

Building passive income streams comes with risks. Investments can go down as well as up, and there is always the possibility of losing money. However, there are steps you can take to manage risks and protect your assets.

Diversification is one of the most effective ways to manage risk. By investing in multiple assets across different industries and asset classes, you can spread your risk and minimize the impact of any one investment underperforming.

Another way to manage risk is to invest in assets that have a history of strong performance and stability. For example, stocks with a long track record of paying dividends may be a safer bet than investing in speculative stocks with high volatility and no earnings history.

It's also important to have a solid understanding of each asset and its potential risks before investing. Take the time to research each investment opportunity thoroughly, and consult with financial professionals if necessary.

Finally, be prepared to make adjustments to your investment strategy as needed. The market and economic conditions are constantly changing, and what may have worked in the past may not work in the future. Stay flexible and be willing to adapt to changing circumstances to protect your assets and ensure long-term success.

In conclusion, building passive income streams is a powerful way to achieve financial independence and create long-term wealth. By choosing the right assets, diversifying your portfolio, and managing risks effectively, you can build a strong foundation of passive income streams that provide a reliable source of cash flow over time. Remember to be patient, stay informed, and stay focused on your long-term financial goals. With dedication and perseverance, you can achieve abundance and success through the

power of passive income.

INVESTING IN YOURSELF

Chapter 8

Investing in yourself is one of the most important investments you can make for your life. When you invest in your personal development, education, and skills, you set yourself up for long-term success and abundance. In this chapter, we will discuss the value of personal development, investing in your education and skills, and the impact of self-care on wealth creation.

The Value of Personal Development

Personal development is the process of improving yourself through various activities, such as reading, learning, or self-reflection. When you commit to personal development, you create an opportunity to grow and evolve into the best version of yourself. Personal development helps you to identify your strengths and weaknesses, your values, and your purpose. It enables you to set goals and to work towards them with focus and intention.

Personal development is essential for building an abundance mindset. By focusing on growth and development, you shift your attention from scarcity and lack to abundance and opportunity. You become more resilient, adaptable, and creative, and you approach challenges with a positive attitude.

Investing in Your Education and Skills

Investing in your education and skills is one of the most valuable investments you can make. Education and skills are assets that stay with you throughout your life and can open doors to opportunities and wealth.

There are many ways to invest in your education and skills, such as taking courses, attending workshops or conferences, or pursuing higher education. The key is to invest in areas that align with your interests and goals and that have the potential to add value to your life and career.

When you invest in your education and skills, you increase your knowledge and expertise, which can lead to better job opportunities, higher salaries, and increased earning potential. You also become more valuable to your employer, and you may be more likely to receive promotions or advancements.

The Impact of Self Care on Wealth Creation

Self-care is the practice of taking care of yourself physically, mentally, and emotionally. Self-care is essential for wealth creation because it helps you to maintain your health, well-being, and energy, which are critical for success.

Self-care includes activities such as exercise, healthy eating, getting enough sleep, and taking time to relax and recharge. It also includes practices such as meditation, mindfulness, and gratitude, which help to reduce stress and increase resilience.

Self-care is often overlooked in the pursuit of wealth and success, but it is essential for long-term sustainability. When you neglect self-care, you risk burnout, illness, and diminished performance.

By prioritizing self-care, you maintain your health and well-being, which allows you to perform at your best and to achieve your goals with greater ease and enjoyment.

In conclusion, investing in yourself is a critical component of attracting wealth and abundance into your life. By committing to personal development, investing in your education and skills, and prioritizing self-care, you set yourself up for long-term success and fulfillment. Remember, you are your most valuable asset, so take the time to invest in yourself and watch your abundance grow.

NETWORKING AND THE POWER OF CONNECTIONS

Chapter 9

In today's world, building a strong network is essential to achieving success and attracting abundance. Whether you are an entrepreneur, business owner, or simply looking to advance your career, your ability to make meaningful connections can open up a world of opportunities. In this chapter, we will explore the importance of building a strong network, strategies for effective networking, and how to leverage connections for abundance.

The Importance of Building a Strong Network

Your network is one of the most valuable assets you have in your pursuit of abundance. It is the people you know and the relationships you have built that can provide you with the support, guidance, and opportunities you need to achieve your goals. A strong network can help you:

1. **Access new opportunities**: The people in your network may have access to job openings, business opportunities, or other resources that can help you achieve your goals.

2. **Gain valuable insights**: Your network can provide you with valuable insights into industries, markets, and trends that can help you make better decisions.

3. **Develop new skills**: Your network can connect you with mentors and experts who can help you develop new skills and knowledge.

4. **Receive support**: Your network can provide you with emotional support and encouragement when facing challenges.

Strategies for Effective Networking

Networking can seem daunting, but it doesn't have to be. By following a few key strategies, you can build a strong network that will help you achieve your goals.

1. **Be genuine**: People can sense when you are being insincere. When networking, focus on building genuine connections with others rather than just trying to get something from them.

2. **Attend events**: Attend networking events in your industry or community to meet new people and expand your network.

3. **Join groups**: Join groups or organizations related to your interests or profession to meet like-minded individuals.

4. **Utilize social media**: Social media platforms like LinkedIn can be great tools for networking. Connect with people in your industry or profession and engage with them regularly.

5. **Follow up**: After meeting someone, be sure to follow up with them to keep the relationship alive. This could be as simple as sending an email or connecting on social media.

Leveraging Connections for Abundance

Once you have built a strong network, it's time to leverage those connections to achieve abundance. Here are some tips for doing just that:

1. **Be clear about your goals**: When reaching out to your network, be clear about what you are looking for and how others can help you.

2. **Provide value**: Networking is a two-way street. Be sure to offer value to those in your network by sharing your expertise, providing referrals, or offering to help in any way you can.

3. **Ask for introductions**: If there is someone you would like to connect with, don't be afraid to ask for an introduction from someone in your network.

4. **Stay in touch**: It's important to stay in touch with your network even when you don't need anything. This could

be as simple as sending a friendly email or sharing an interesting article.

5. **Be grateful**: When someone in your network helps you achieve your goals, be sure to express your gratitude. A simple thank you can go a long way in strengthening the relationship.

In conclusion, building a strong network is essential to attracting abundance in your life. By following these strategies for effective networking and leveraging your connections, you can open up a world of opportunities and achieve your goals. Remember to be genuine, attend events, join groups, utilize social media, and follow up. By doing so, you can cultivate a network that will support you on your journey toward greater wealth and success.

CULTIVATING AN ABUNDANCE MINDSET

Chapter 10

In this chapter, we will explore the concept of cultivating an abundance mindset, which is an essential ingredient for attracting wealth and abundance into your life. We will discuss how to recognize and overcome scarcity mindset patterns, the techniques for developing an abundance mindset, and daily practices to maintain a positive outlook.

Recognizing Scarcity Mindset Patterns

The first step in cultivating an abundance mindset is to recognize scarcity mindset patterns. Scarcity mindset is a limiting belief that there is never enough of what we need or want. This mindset is based on fear and often results in anxiety, stress, and a lack of fulfillment.

Some common signs of scarcity mindset include constantly worrying about money, feeling jealous or envious of others' success, feeling like you never have enough time or resources, and feeling overwhelmed by responsibilities.

To overcome scarcity mindset, it is important to identify and challenge your limiting beliefs. Ask yourself if your thoughts and beliefs are based on reality or if they are just assumptions that you have made. Are your beliefs empowering or limiting you? Recognizing and challenging these beliefs is the first step towards developing an abundance mindset.

Techniques for Developing an Abundance Mindset

Once you have identified and challenged your scarcity mindset patterns, the next step is to develop an abundance mindset. An abundance mindset is a belief that there is always enough of what you need or want and that there is an unlimited supply of opportunities.

The following techniques can help you cultivate an abundance mindset:

1. **Gratitude**: Practicing gratitude is one of the most powerful ways to cultivate an abundance mindset. By focusing on what you are grateful for, you shift your focus from what you lack to what you have. Make a list of things you are grateful for every day, no matter how small they may seem.

2. **Visualization**: Visualization is a technique that involves using your imagination to create a mental picture of what you want to achieve. Visualize yourself living the life you desire and experiencing the feelings of joy and abundance that come with it.

3. **Affirmations**: Affirmations are positive statements that you repeat to yourself daily to reinforce positive beliefs. Use affirmations that reflect your goals and desires, such as "I am worthy of abundance and success," or "I attract wealth and prosperity into my life."

4. **Positive self-talk**: The way you talk to yourself can have a significant impact on your mindset. Practice positive self-talk by reframing negative thoughts into positive ones. For example, instead of saying "I'll never be able to afford that," say "I am capable of finding a way to afford that."

5. **Surround yourself with positivity**: Surround yourself with people who have an abundance mindset and who inspire and motivate you. Read books and listen to podcasts that focus on personal growth and abundance.

Daily Practices to Maintain a Positive Outlook

Cultivating an abundance mindset is an ongoing process that requires daily practice. Here are some daily practices to maintain a positive outlook:

1. **Start your day with positivity**: Begin your day with a positive affirmation, visualization, or gratitude practice. This sets a positive tone for the day ahead.

2. **Practice mindfulness**: Mindfulness is a technique that involves being fully present in the moment without judgment. Practice mindfulness through meditation, deep breathing, or simply being aware of your surroundings.

3. **Set goals**: Set SMART (specific, measurable, achievable, relevant, and time-bound) goals that align with your values and desires. Focus on taking small steps towards your goals every day.

4. **Take care of yourself**: Self-care is essential for maintaining a positive outlook. Take care of your physical, emotional, and mental health through exercise, healthy eating, rest, and relaxation.

5. **Celebrate successes**: Celebrating your successes reinforces positive beliefs and encourages you to continue taking steps towards your goals.

6. **Practice generosity**: Giving to others is a powerful way

to cultivate an abundance mindset. Practice generosity by volunteering, donating to charity, or simply being kind and helpful to those around you.

7. **Reflect on your progress**: Take time to reflect on your progress and celebrate your successes. Reflecting on how far you have come can help you stay motivated and maintain a positive outlook.

By incorporating these daily practices into your life, you can maintain a positive outlook and cultivate an abundance mindset. Remember that developing an abundance mindset is an ongoing process and requires consistent effort and practice.

In conclusion, cultivating an abundance mindset is essential for attracting wealth and abundance into your life. By recognizing and overcoming scarcity mindset patterns, using techniques such as gratitude, visualization, affirmations, and positive self-talk, and practicing daily habits to maintain a positive outlook, you can cultivate an abundance mindset that will help you achieve your goals and create a fulfilling life.

Remember that developing an abundance mindset is a journey, and it requires effort and practice every day. But with dedication and consistency, you can unlock the secrets to abundance and attract wealth and success into your life. So, start cultivating an abundance mindset today and take the first step towards a life of prosperity and fulfillment!

OVERCOMING FEAR
AND TAKING ACTION

Chapter 11

The fear of failure is one of the most significant obstacles to achieving abundance and success in life. Whether it's a fear of rejection, a fear of making mistakes, or a fear of the unknown, these fears can hold us back from taking the necessary action to achieve our goals. In this chapter, we will explore strategies for identifying and overcoming the fears that hold you back, as well as how to embrace failure as a learning opportunity.

Identifying Fears That Hold You Back

The first step in overcoming fear is to identify the specific fears that are holding you back. Often, these fears are subconscious, meaning they are deeply ingrained in our minds and are difficult to recognize. One way to identify your fears is to start paying attention to your thoughts and emotions.

What are the thoughts that run through your mind when you think about taking action toward your goals? Do you feel anxious or fearful? If so, try to pinpoint the specific fear that is causing these emotions. It could be fear of failure, fear of rejection, fear of the unknown, or even fear of success.

Once you have identified your specific fears, you can start to take action to overcome them.

Strategies for Overcoming Fear

There are several strategies that can be effective in overcoming fear.

Here are a few of the most effective:

1. **Face Your Fears** - One of the most effective ways to overcome fear is to face it head-on. This means taking action, even when you feel afraid. By taking action, you are showing yourself that you are capable of overcoming your fears.

2. **Practice Visualization** - Visualization is a powerful

technique for overcoming fear. Take some time each day to visualize yourself taking action toward your goals. Imagine yourself succeeding and achieving the results you desire.

3. **Use Affirmations** - Affirmations are positive statements that you repeat to yourself. They can be an effective way to reprogram your subconscious mind and overcome fear. For example, you might repeat the affirmation, "I am capable of achieving my goals" several times each day.

4. **Take Small Steps** - Taking small steps toward your goals can help you build confidence and overcome fear. Instead of trying to tackle everything at once, break your goals down into smaller, more manageable steps.

Embracing Failure as a Learning Opportunity

One of the biggest fears that hold people back is the fear of failure. However, it's important to recognize that failure is a natural part of the learning process. In fact, many successful people have experienced multiple failures before achieving their goals.

Rather than seeing failure as a negative experience, try to reframe it as a learning opportunity. Ask yourself, "What can I learn from this experience?" or "How can I use this experience to improve?"

By embracing failure as a learning opportunity, you can turn what might have been a negative experience into a positive one. You can use your failures to gain valuable insights that can help you achieve even greater success in the future.

Overcoming fear is a critical step in achieving abundance and success in life. By identifying your specific fears, using strategies to overcome them, and embracing failure as a learning opportunity, you can take the necessary action to achieve your goals.

Remember, everyone experiences fear at some point in their lives. The key is to not let fear hold you back from achieving your full potential. With practice, you can learn to overcome your fears and take the necessary action to achieve your goals.

THE ROLE OF MONEY MANAGEMENT

Chapter 12

Money management is a crucial element in achieving abundance and prosperity in life. It is not just about earning more money, but also about how to manage and use it effectively. In this chapter, we will explore the importance of developing healthy money habits, creating and maintaining a budget, and the power of compound interest.

Developing Healthy Money Habits

Developing healthy money habits is crucial in achieving abundance and wealth. It involves creating a mindset that sees money as a tool for achieving your goals rather than a source of stress and anxiety. It requires discipline, consistency, and patience.

Healthy money habits include:

1. **Tracking your expenses**: Keeping track of your expenses helps you identify areas where you may be overspending and make adjustments to your budget.

2. **Saving regularly**: Consistently saving a percentage of your income helps you build a cushion for emergencies and long-term goals.

3. **Avoiding debt**: Avoiding debt helps you avoid the stress and burden of paying high-interest rates.

4. **Investing wisely**: Investing your money in assets that appreciate in value over time can help you grow your wealth.

Creating and Maintaining a Budget

Creating and maintaining a budget is a key element of effective money management. It helps you keep track of your income and expenses, prioritize your spending, and avoid overspending.

Here are the steps to create and maintain a budget:

1. **Determine your income**: Calculate your monthly income, including your salary, bonuses, and any other sources of income.

2. **List your expenses**: List all your expenses, including fixed expenses like rent, utilities, and insurance, and variable expenses like groceries, entertainment, and travel.

3. **Categorize your expenses**: Categorize your expenses into necessary and discretionary expenses. Necessary expenses are essential for your basic needs, while discretionary expenses are for non-essential items.

4. **Prioritize your spending**: Prioritize your spending by allocating your income to necessary expenses first and then discretionary expenses based on their importance.

5. **Monitor your spending**: Monitor your spending regularly to ensure that you are staying within your budget.

The Power of Compound Interest

Compound interest is the interest earned on both the principal amount and the interest earned on it over time. It is a powerful tool for building wealth and achieving abundance.

Here's how it works:

Let's say you invest $1,000 at a 5% annual interest rate. After one year, you will have earned $50 in interest. If you reinvest the interest, the new principal amount will be $1,050, and after the second year, you will earn $52.50 in interest. The interest earned in the second year is not only on the original principal of $1,000 but also on the interest earned in the first year, which is $50.

Over time, the power of compound interest can help your investments grow exponentially. The key is to start early, invest consistently, and reinvest the interest earned.

In conclusion, money management is a critical element in achieving abundance and prosperity in life. Developing healthy money habits, creating and maintaining a budget, and understanding the power of compound interest are essential tools for building wealth and achieving your financial goals. By applying these principles in your life, you can take control of your finances and achieve greater abundance and success.

THE LAW OF ABUNDANCE AND RELATIONSHIPS

Chapter 13

Human beings are social creatures. We thrive on connections and relationships, and our lives are often shaped by the people we choose to surround ourselves with. Relationships play a vital role in our overall well-being, including our financial health. In this chapter, we will explore how to attract abundant relationships, the impact of relationships on wealth creation, and how to cultivate healthy partnerships.

Attracting Abundant Relationships

Just like anything else in life, attracting abundant relationships begins with mindset. If you believe that you are deserving of healthy, supportive relationships, you are more likely to attract them into your life. On the other hand, if you have limiting beliefs about relationships, such as "I always attract toxic people," you may find yourself in a pattern of unhealthy relationships.

To attract abundant relationships, start by focusing on the positive aspects of your existing relationships. Look for the qualities you admire in others, and strive to embody those qualities yourself. Be open to meeting new people and building connections, and practice empathy and compassion in all of your interactions.

It's also important to remember that abundance in relationships doesn't necessarily mean having a large circle of friends or a romantic partner. Abundance can also manifest in the quality of your relationships, such as having a few close friends who truly understand and support you.

The Impact of Relationships on Wealth Creation

Our relationships can have a significant impact on our financial health. For example, if you have a close friend or family member who is financially successful, they may be able to provide guidance or connections that can help you in your own career or business endeavors.

On the other hand, if you surround yourself with people who have a negative or scarcity mindset when it comes to money, you may find yourself adopting those same beliefs and struggling to achieve financial abundance.

It's important to be mindful of the energy that your relationships bring into your life. Surround yourself with people who uplift and inspire you, and limit your time with those who drain your energy or bring negativity into your life.

Cultivating Healthy Partnerships

When it comes to romantic relationships, it's important to remember that wealth and success are not the only factors that contribute to a healthy partnership. Communication, trust, and mutual respect are essential components of a strong relationship.

It's also important to approach relationships from a place of abundance, rather than scarcity. This means recognizing that there are plenty of potential partners out there, and that you are deserving of a relationship that brings you joy and fulfillment.

When you do find a partner who aligns with your values and supports your goals, it's important to nurture that relationship with care and intention. Practice active listening, express gratitude and appreciation, and make time for quality moments together.

Relationships are an integral part of our lives, and they play a significant role in our overall well-being, including our financial health. By cultivating an abundance mindset and focusing on building healthy, supportive relationships, we can attract the right people into our lives and create a community of like-minded individuals who are committed to growth and success.

Remember, abundance in relationships doesn't necessarily mean having a large circle of friends or a romantic partner. It's about quality over quantity, and surrounding ourselves with people who uplift and inspire us.

In the next chapter, we will explore the power of intuition and how it can help us make more aligned and successful decisions in all areas of our lives.

HARNESSING THE POWER OF INTUITION

Chapter 14

Have you ever had a gut feeling that turned out to be right? Or perhaps you had a hunch that led to a positive outcome? These experiences are examples of the power of intuition, which can be a valuable tool in attracting abundance into your life. In this chapter, we will explore the role of intuition in wealth creation and how you can develop and trust your intuition to make intuitive decisions for abundance.

Understanding the Role of Intuition

Intuition is often described as a "gut feeling" or a sense of inner knowing that arises without logical reasoning. It is a subconscious process that enables us to make quick decisions based on our experiences, knowledge, and emotions. Intuition can be a powerful source of insight and guidance, especially in situations where there is no clear answer or when we need to make a quick decision.

When it comes to attracting abundance, intuition plays an important role. Often, our intuition will guide us towards opportunities and paths that align with our desires and values. By learning to trust and follow our intuition, we can tap into the abundance that the universe has to offer.

Developing Intuition through Meditation and Mindfulness

One way to develop intuition is through the practice of meditation and mindfulness. By quieting the mind and focusing on the present moment, we can tune into our inner guidance and strengthen our intuition. Meditation and mindfulness also help us to become more aware of our thoughts and emotions, which can aid in identifying limiting beliefs or negative patterns that may be blocking abundance.

To start developing your intuition through meditation, find a quiet place to sit comfortably and set a timer for 10-15 minutes. Close your eyes and focus on your breath, allowing your thoughts to come and go without judgment. If you find your mind wandering, gently bring your attention back to your breath. With regular practice, you may start to notice intuitive insights or flashes of inspiration that arise during or after your meditation practice.

Making Intuitive Decisions for Abundance

Once you have developed your intuition, it's important to trust it and use it to make intuitive decisions that align with your goals and values. This can be particularly helpful when it comes to attracting abundance, as our intuition can guide us towards opportunities and paths that are in our best interest.

To make intuitive decisions for abundance, start by setting clear intentions and visualizing your desired outcome. Then, pay attention to any intuitive insights or guidance that arises. This may come in the form of a hunch, a feeling, or an inner knowing. Trust that your intuition knows what is best for you and follow its guidance, even if it doesn't seem logical or rational at the time.

It's important to note that intuition should not be used as a substitute for critical thinking or analysis. Instead, it should be used in conjunction with these skills to make well-informed decisions that are also in alignment with your intuition.

Harnessing the power of intuition is a valuable tool in attracting abundance into your life. By developing and trusting your intuition, you can tap into the abundance that the universe has to offer and make intuitive decisions that align with your goals and values. Through the practice of meditation and mindfulness, you can strengthen your intuition and become more aware of the insights and guidance that arise. Remember to set clear intentions and visualize your desired outcome, and trust that your intuition knows what is best for you. With practice, you can make intuitive decisions for abundance and attract wealth and success into your life.

THE SPIRITUAL SIDE
OF ABUNDANCE

Chapter 15

The Law of Abundance is not only about attracting wealth and success into your life. It is also about understanding the deeper spiritual principles that underpin abundance. In this chapter, we will explore the connection between spirituality and wealth, and how you can tap into your spiritual side to attract abundance into your life.

The Connection Between
Spirituality and Wealth

Many people believe that spirituality and wealth are mutually exclusive concepts. They think that money and material possessions are superficial and that true happiness and fulfillment come from living a simple life. While it is true that material possessions do not guarantee happiness, it is also true that money and abundance can be used to create positive change in the world.

Spirituality and wealth are not mutually exclusive. In fact, many spiritual traditions teach that abundance is a natural byproduct of living in alignment with your higher purpose. When you align your thoughts, beliefs, and actions with your highest values and purpose, you create a powerful flow of energy that attracts abundance into your life.

Practicing Mindfulness and Meditation for Abundance

Mindfulness and meditation are powerful tools for cultivating an abundance mindset. Mindfulness is the practice of being present and fully engaged in the moment, without judgment or distraction. Meditation is the practice of training your mind to focus and quiet your thoughts.

By practicing mindfulness and meditation, you can develop a deeper awareness of your thoughts, emotions, and beliefs. You can also cultivate a sense of inner peace and calm, which can help you to stay centered and focused in the face of challenges.

Meditation can also help you to tap into the power of the Universe. When you meditate, you create a space for the Universe to communicate with you. This can help you to gain insights and clarity about your life purpose, and to receive guidance on how to attract abundance into your life.

Embracing Your Higher Purpose

At the core of the Law of Abundance is the idea that each of us has a unique purpose in life. When we live in alignment with that purpose, we create a powerful flow of energy that attracts abundance into our lives.

To discover your higher purpose, ask yourself what brings you the most joy and fulfillment. What activities or experiences leave you feeling energized and inspired? What skills or talents do you have that you enjoy using?

Once you have identified your higher purpose, make it the focus of your life. Align your thoughts, beliefs, and actions with your purpose, and take inspired action to bring your vision into reality. This may involve making changes in your career, relationships, or lifestyle, but the rewards will be well worth it.

In conclusion, the Law of Abundance is not just about attracting wealth and success into your life. It is also about tapping into your spiritual side and living in alignment with your higher purpose. By practicing mindfulness and meditation, and by embracing your higher purpose, you can create a powerful flow of energy that attracts abundance into your life.

Remember, abundance is not just about money and material possessions. It is about living a rich and fulfilling life that is aligned with your deepest values and purpose. So take the time to connect with your spiritual side, and watch as abundance flows into your life in ways you never imagined possible.

THE IMPACT OF
ENVIRONMENT
ON WEALTH

Chapter 16

The environment we surround ourselves with can have a significant impact on our mindset, our productivity, and ultimately, our wealth. When we create an environment that fosters success, we set ourselves up for abundance and prosperity. In this chapter, we will explore the influence of surroundings on mindset, the importance of creating an environment that supports our goals, and how leveraging Feng Shui can enhance abundance in our lives.

The Influence of Surroundings on Mindset

Our surroundings have a powerful effect on our mindset. When we are in an environment that is cluttered, chaotic, and disorganized, it can be challenging to focus on our goals and stay motivated. On the other hand, when we are in a clean, well-organized space, we are more likely to feel energized, productive, and focused.

The environment we create for ourselves also impacts our mood and emotions. If we are constantly surrounded by negativity, it can be challenging to maintain a positive outlook on life. Alternatively, if we surround ourselves with positivity, we are more likely to maintain a positive mindset, even in the face of adversity.

Creating an Environment that Fosters Success

Creating an environment that fosters success is essential if we want to attract wealth and abundance into our lives. The first step is to declutter and organize our physical space. A cluttered environment can be overwhelming and make it challenging to focus on our goals. By decluttering and organizing our space, we free up mental energy and create a clear path for success.

Next, we should surround ourselves with things that inspire us and support our goals. This might include artwork that inspires creativity, motivational quotes, or even plants that purify the air and bring a sense of calmness to the space. By surrounding ourselves with things that inspire us, we create an environment that supports our success.

Finally, we should create a workspace that is optimized for productivity. This might mean investing in a comfortable chair and desk or setting up a dedicated workspace that is free from distractions. By creating a workspace that is optimized for productivity, we set ourselves up for success and make it easier to achieve our goals.

Leveraging Feng Shui for Abundance

Feng Shui is an ancient Chinese practice that involves arranging our physical environment in a way that promotes balance and harmony. The principles of Feng Shui can be applied to our homes and workspaces to enhance abundance and prosperity in our lives.

One of the key principles of Feng Shui is the placement of objects and furniture. For example, the location of our bed, desk, and other furniture can impact our energy levels and productivity. By positioning our furniture in a way that is aligned with the principles of Feng Shui, we can create an environment that supports our goals and enhances abundance in our lives.

Another key principle of Feng Shui is the use of colors. Different colors can impact our mood and energy levels. For example, red is associated with energy and passion, while blue is associated with calmness and tranquility. By incorporating colors that are aligned with our goals, we can enhance the energy of our environment and attract abundance into our lives.

In conclusion, the environment we create for ourselves has a significant impact on our mindset, productivity, and ultimately, our wealth. By creating an environment that fosters success, we set ourselves up for abundance and prosperity. We can achieve this by decluttering and organizing our space, surrounding ourselves with things that inspire us, and creating a workspace that is optimized for productivity. We can also leverage the principles of Feng Shui to enhance abundance in our lives. By aligning our physical environment with the principles of Feng Shui, we can create an environment that supports our goals and attracts wealth and prosperity into our lives.

TIME MANAGEMENT AND PRODUCTIVITY

Chapter 17

In today's fast-paced world, time is a valuable resource. Many people find themselves struggling to balance work, family, and personal commitments, leaving them feeling overwhelmed and stressed. However, effective time management and productivity strategies can help individuals achieve more in less time, leading to greater success and abundance.

The Importance of Effective Time Management

Effective time management is essential for achieving success and abundance. Time is a limited resource, and once it's gone, it cannot be regained. Therefore, it's crucial to use time wisely to maximize productivity and achieve goals.

Effective time management can help individuals to:

1. **Reduce stress**: By managing time efficiently, individuals can reduce stress levels and feel more in control of their lives.

2. **Increase productivity**: Effective time management can help individuals to complete tasks more efficiently, allowing them to accomplish more in less time.

3. **Achieve goals**: By prioritizing tasks and managing time effectively, individuals can achieve their goals more quickly and efficiently.

2. **Improve work-life balance**: With effective time management, individuals can balance their work and personal lives, leading to greater overall satisfaction and abundance.

Strategies for Increasing Productivity

There are many strategies that individuals can use to increase productivity and make the most of their time.

Here are a few techniques to try:

1. **Set SMART goals**: SMART goals are specific, measurable, achievable, relevant, and time-bound. Setting SMART goals can help individuals to stay focused and motivated, leading to greater productivity.

2. **Prioritize tasks**: Prioritizing tasks can help individuals to focus on the most important and urgent tasks, allowing them to complete them first and avoid procrastination.

3. **Use a calendar**: Using a calendar or planner can help individuals to stay organized and manage their time effectively. By scheduling tasks and appointments, individuals can avoid double-booking and stay on track.

4. **Break tasks into smaller chunks**: Large tasks can be overwhelming, leading to procrastination and decreased productivity. Breaking tasks into smaller, more manageable chunks can make them more approachable and easier to complete.

5. **Take breaks**: Taking regular breaks can help individuals to recharge and refocus, leading to greater productivity and creativity.

6. **Avoid multitasking**: Multitasking can actually decrease productivity and increase stress levels. Instead, focus on one task at a time and give it your full attention.

Prioritizing Tasks for Optimal Results

One of the most important aspects of effective time management is prioritizing tasks for optimal results.

Here are a few tips to help prioritize tasks:

1. **Use the Eisenhower Matrix**: The Eisenhower Matrix is a tool that helps individuals to categorize tasks based on their urgency and importance. Tasks can be classified as either urgent and important, important but not urgent, urgent but not important, or neither urgent nor important. This can help individuals to prioritize tasks and focus on the most

important and urgent ones first.

2. **Consider the impact**: When prioritizing tasks, consider the impact each task will have on achieving your goals. Focus on the tasks that will have the greatest impact on achieving your goals.

3. **Consider deadlines**: Tasks with impending deadlines should be prioritized to ensure they are completed on time.

4. **Be realistic**: It's important to be realistic when prioritizing tasks. Avoid overloading your schedule with too many tasks and focus on what is achievable within the given time frame.

Effective time management and productivity strategies are essential for achieving abundance and success. By managing time effectively and prioritizing tasks, individuals can reduce stress, increase productivity, achieve goals, and improve their work-life balance. Using tools like the Eisenhower Matrix and setting SMART goals can help individuals to stay focused and motivated, leading to greater productivity and abundance. Remember, time is a valuable resource, so use it wisely to achieve your goals and fulfill your dreams. By prioritizing tasks and managing time effectively, you can create a life of abundance and success. Remember, it's never too late to start managing your time and increasing your productivity. With the right mindset and strategies, you can achieve anything you set your mind to.

Incorporating these strategies into your daily routine can take time and effort, but the benefits are worth it. By being intentional with your time and prioritizing tasks, you can achieve more in less time, allowing you to focus on the things that matter most. Remember to take breaks and avoid multitasking, as these can decrease productivity and increase stress levels.

It's also important to be flexible and adaptable when it comes to managing your time. Unexpected events and distractions can arise, so it's important to be able to adjust your schedule and priorities accordingly. By being proactive and flexible, you can manage your time effectively and achieve your goals.

In summary, effective time management and productivity strategies are essential for achieving abundance and success. By prioritizing tasks, setting SMART goals, using tools like the Eisenhower Matrix, and taking breaks, you can increase productivity, reduce stress, and achieve your goals. Remember to be flexible and adaptable, and don't be afraid to ask for help when needed. With the right mindset and strategies, you can create a life of abundance and success.

EMBRACING CHANGE AND ADAPTABILITY

Chapter 18

Change is a constant in life, and it's inevitable. In order to attract wealth and abundance into your life, it's crucial to understand that embracing change is a key component of achieving success. Change can be both exciting and terrifying, but the ability to adapt and be resilient in the face of challenges is essential. In this chapter, we'll explore the importance of embracing change and developing adaptability and resilience, as well as how to turn obstacles into opportunities.

The Inevitability of Change

Change can come in many forms, whether it's a new job, a relationship ending, a move to a new city, or a shift in personal circumstances. It's important to recognize that change is a natural part of life and that it's impossible to avoid entirely.

Fighting against change can lead to stress, anxiety, and missed opportunities. Embracing change, on the other hand, can bring new possibilities and experiences that can lead to growth and abundance.

Developing Adaptability and Resilience

Adaptability and resilience are important traits to develop in order to thrive in a world that is constantly changing. Adaptability means being able to adjust to new situations and challenges quickly and effectively, while resilience is the ability to bounce back from setbacks and failures. These skills can be developed through practice and by embracing a growth mindset.

One way to develop adaptability and resilience is to step outside of your comfort zone and try new things. This can be as simple as trying a new hobby or as challenging as taking on a new job or moving to a new city. Embracing change and taking calculated risks can help build confidence and resilience.

Another way to develop these skills is to focus on problem-solving. When faced with a challenge or obstacle, instead of getting discouraged, look for ways to overcome it. Break the problem down into smaller, manageable pieces and come up with a plan to tackle each one. This process can help build adaptability and resilience by teaching you to be proactive and to view setbacks as opportunities for growth.

Turning Obstacles into Opportunities

Obstacles can be viewed as roadblocks or as opportunities for growth. When faced with a challenge, it's important to take a step back and assess the situation objectively. Ask yourself, "What can I learn from this?" or "How can I turn this into an opportunity?"

One way to turn obstacles into opportunities is to focus on solutions rather than problems. Instead of dwelling on the negative aspects of a situation, look for ways to overcome it. This can involve seeking out resources, collaborating with others, or re-framing the situation in a positive light.

Another way to turn obstacles into opportunities is to focus on the bigger picture. Ask yourself, "What is the ultimate goal?" or "What do I want to achieve?" By keeping your end goal in mind, you can stay motivated and focused on finding solutions rather than getting bogged down by setbacks.

Embracing change and developing adaptability and resilience are essential components of attracting wealth and abundance into your life. Change is inevitable, and the ability to adapt and be resilient in the face of challenges can lead to new opportunities and experiences. By focusing on solutions rather than problems and keeping the bigger picture in mind, you can turn obstacles into opportunities for growth and success.

THE POWER OF POSITIVE THINKING

Chapter 19

When it comes to attracting abundance and wealth into your life, one of the most powerful tools at your disposal is your own mindset. Your thoughts, beliefs, and attitudes have a tremendous impact on the world around you, shaping your experiences and influencing the opportunities that come your way.

This is where the power of positive thinking comes into play. By cultivating a mindset of optimism and positivity, you can tap into the limitless potential of the universe and unlock new levels of abundance and success in your life.

In this chapter, we will explore the science behind positive thinking, as well as some techniques for cultivating a more optimistic mindset and overcoming negativity and self-doubt.

The Science Behind Positive Thinking

At its core, positive thinking is about harnessing the power of your thoughts and emotions to create a more positive and fulfilling reality. This may sound like a New Age concept, but it is actually backed up by a growing body of scientific research.

For example, studies have shown that people who practice positive thinking tend to have lower levels of stress, better physical health, and greater overall happiness and life satisfaction. They are also more likely to succeed in their personal and professional goals, as their optimistic mindset allows them to overcome obstacles and stay motivated even in the face of setbacks.

One reason for this is that positive thinking helps to rewire the brain, creating new neural pathways and strengthening the connections between different regions of the brain. This can lead to greater creativity, improved problem-solving skills, and better memory and learning abilities.

Positive thinking is also closely linked to the Law of Attraction, which states that we attract into our lives whatever we focus our thoughts and emotions on. By maintaining a positive mindset and visualizing the abundance and success that you desire, you can begin to manifest these things into your reality.

Techniques for Cultivating Optimism

So how can you cultivate a more optimistic mindset and tap into the power of positive thinking?

Here are a few techniques that can help:

1. **Practice gratitude**. One of the simplest and most effective ways to shift your mindset toward positivity is to focus on the things in your life that you are grateful for. Make a daily habit of listing three things that you are thankful for, no matter how small or seemingly insignificant they may be.

2. **Reframe negative thoughts**. When you find yourself thinking negative thoughts, try to reframe them in a more

positive light. For example, instead of thinking "I'll never be able to do this," try thinking "I may face some challenges, but I am capable of finding a way to overcome them."

3. **Visualize success**. Spend some time each day visualizing the success and abundance that you desire. Imagine yourself living the life of your dreams, feeling happy, fulfilled, and abundant in every way.

4. **Surround yourself with positivity**. Seek out positive influences in your life, such as supportive friends and family members, uplifting books and media, and inspiring mentors and role models.

Overcoming Negativity and Self Doubt

Even the most optimistic and positive-minded individuals may face moments of doubt and negativity from time to time. The key is to recognize these thoughts and feelings for what they are and take steps to overcome them.

Here are a few techniques for dealing with negativity and self-doubt:

1. **Practice self-compassion**. When you are feeling negative or down on yourself, practice self-compassion by treating yourself with kindness and understanding. Remember that everyone makes mistakes and faces challenges from time to time.

2. **Challenge negative self-talk**. When you find yourself thinking negative thoughts about yourself or your abilities, challenge them by asking yourself if they are really true. Often, our negative thoughts are based on false beliefs or assumptions that can be easily debunked.

3. **Take action**. Sometimes, the best way to overcome negativity and self-doubt is simply to take action. By taking small steps toward your goals and building momentum over time, you can prove to yourself that you are capable of achieving great things.

4. **Seek support**. Don't be afraid to reach out to friends, family members, or a trusted professional if you are struggling with negativity or self-doubt. Sometimes, talking through your feelings with someone else can help you gain a new perspective and find solutions to your challenges.

The power of positive thinking is a potent force for attracting abundance and wealth into your life. By cultivating a mindset of optimism and positivity, you can tap into the limitless potential of the universe and manifest your dreams into reality.

Remember that positive thinking is not about ignoring the challenges and difficulties in your life, but rather about approaching them with a mindset of possibility and growth. With practice and dedication, you can transform your thoughts and emotions to create a more abundant and fulfilling life.

In the next chapter, we will explore the importance of time management and productivity in achieving your goals and unlocking the secrets to abundance.

PUTTING IT ALL TOGETHER

Chapter 20

Congratulations on reaching the final chapter of this book on the Law of Abundance! By now, you should have gained a thorough understanding of the principles of abundance and the power of mindset, beliefs, gratitude, visualization, goal-setting, giving, investing in yourself, networking, intuition, spirituality, and positive thinking in attracting wealth and abundance into your life.

In this chapter, we will bring together all the principles we have discussed and help you create a personalized plan for wealth attraction. We will also discuss how to maintain momentum and hold yourself accountable for your progress.

Reviewing Key Principles of Abundance

Before we move on, let's do a quick recap of the key principles of abundance that we have covered in this book:

1. **Abundance and wealth**: Abundance refers to the state of having more than enough of what you need or desire, while wealth is the accumulation of resources that have value in society, such as money, property, and investments.

2. **Mindset**: Your mindset is the way you think about yourself, others, and the world. An abundance mindset involves a positive and optimistic outlook on life, a belief in your ability to achieve your goals, and a willingness to take risks and embrace opportunities.

3. **Belief**: Your beliefs shape your reality by influencing your thoughts, feelings, and actions. Limiting beliefs can hold you back from reaching your full potential, while empowering beliefs can help you achieve your goals.

4. **Visualization and affirmations**: Visualization involves

creating a mental image of what you want to achieve, while affirmations are positive statements that help you reinforce empowering beliefs and overcome limiting beliefs.

5. **Gratitude and the Law of Attraction**: Gratitude is the practice of appreciating what you have, and the Law of Attraction is the idea that you attract into your life what you focus on.

6. **Goal-setting**: Setting specific, measurable, achievable, relevant, and time-bound (SMART) goals that align with your values and taking action towards them is essential for achieving abundance.

7. **Giving and receiving**: Generosity and reciprocity are important for attracting wealth and abundance. Giving without expecting anything in return can create positive energy and attract more abundance into your life.

8. **Passive income**: Passive income streams, such as rental

income, dividend income, and online business income, can generate wealth without requiring active work.

10. **Investing in yourself**: Personal development, education, skills, and self-care are crucial for wealth creation and personal growth.

11. **Networking and connections**: Building a strong network and leveraging connections can help you create new opportunities and attract wealth and abundance.

12. **Abundance mindset**: Recognizing and overcoming scarcity mindset patterns and practicing daily habits to maintain a positive outlook are essential for developing an abundance mindset.

13. **Overcoming fear and taking action**: Identifying and overcoming fears that hold you back and embracing failure as a learning opportunity can help you take action towards your goals.

14. **Money management**: Developing healthy money habits, creating and maintaining a budget, and understanding the power of compound interest are important for building wealth.

15. **Abundance and relationships**: Attracting and cultivating healthy relationships can have a positive impact on your wealth creation journey.

16. **Intuition**: Developing intuition through mindfulness and meditation and making intuitive decisions can help you achieve abundance.

17. **Spiritual side of abundance**: Practicing mindfulness, meditation, and embracing your higher purpose can help you connect with the spiritual side of abundance.

18. **Environment**: Your surroundings and environment can have an impact on your mindset. Creating an environment that fosters success and leveraging Feng Shui principles can

attract abundance.

19. **Time management and productivity**: Effective time management, increasing productivity, and prioritizing tasks can help you achieve your goals efficiently.

20. **Embracing change and adaptability**: Change is inevitable, and developing adaptability and resilience can help you turn obstacles into opportunities.

21. **Putting it all together**: Now that we have reviewed the key principles of abundance, it's time to create a personalized plan for wealth attraction.

Creating a Personalized Plan for Wealth Attraction

To create a personalized plan for wealth attraction, you need to understand your goals, values, strengths, weaknesses, opportunities, and threats. You also need to identify the specific actions you need to take to achieve your goals.

Here are some steps you can take to create a personalized plan for wealth attraction:

1. **Define your goals**: Start by identifying your long-term and short-term goals, both personal and professional. Make sure they align with your values and are SMART.

2. **Evaluate your current situation**: Assess your current financial situation, including your income, expenses, debts, and assets. Identify your strengths and weaknesses, opportunities, and threats.

3. **Identify your limiting beliefs**: Reflect on your beliefs about money, success, and abundance. Identify any limiting beliefs that may be holding you back.

4. **Develop empowering beliefs**: Create a list of empowering beliefs that will help you overcome limiting beliefs and achieve your goals.

5. **Visualize your ideal future**: Use visualization techniques

to create a mental picture of your ideal future. Imagine yourself living the life you desire and experiencing abundance in all areas of your life.

6. **Take action**: Develop an action plan that includes specific steps you need to take to achieve your goals. Break down your goals into smaller, manageable tasks, and set deadlines for each task.

7. **Hold yourself accountable**: Monitor your progress regularly and hold yourself accountable for your actions. Celebrate your successes, learn from your failures, and make adjustments as needed.

Maintaining Momentum and Staying Accountable

Creating a personalized plan for wealth attraction is only the first step. To achieve abundance, you need to maintain momentum and hold yourself accountable for your progress.

Here are some tips to help you stay on track:

1. **Stay focused**: Keep your goals and vision in mind and stay focused on what you want to achieve.

2. **Track your progress**: Monitor your progress regularly and make adjustments as needed. Celebrate your successes and learn from your failures.

3. **Stay motivated**: Stay motivated by reminding yourself of why you want to achieve your goals and the benefits of abundance.

4. **Surround yourself with positive influences**: Surround yourself with positive people who support your goals and aspirations. Avoid negative influences that may discourage you.

5. **Practice self-care**: Take care of yourself physically, mentally, and emotionally. Get enough sleep, eat a healthy diet, exercise regularly, and practice relaxation techniques such as meditation and yoga.

6. **Stay accountable**: Hold yourself accountable for your actions and results. Use a journal or accountability partner to track your progress and keep yourself motivated.

Congratulations on completing this book on the Law of Abundance! By now, you have learned how to attract wealth and abundance into your life by adopting an abundance mindset, developing empowering beliefs, practicing gratitude, visualization, goal-setting, giving, investing in yourself, networking, intuition, spirituality, positive thinking, and other principles of abundance.

Remember, creating a personalized plan for wealth attraction is only the first step. To achieve abundance, you need to maintain momentum, stay motivated, and hold yourself accountable for your progress.

By following the principles and strategies outlined in this book, you can transform your life and unlock the limitless potential that resides within you. You have the power to attract wealth and abundance into your life, so go ahead and take action towards your goals. Thank you for joining me on this incredible journey, and may you continue to attract abundance into your life for years to come!

CONCLUSION

The Law of Abundance is a powerful force that can transform your life in countless ways. Throughout this book, we have explored the key principles of abundance and how they can be applied to attract wealth, success, and fulfillment into your life. Now, as we reach the conclusion of this journey, it is important to reflect on the transformative power of the Law of Abundance and the limitless potential that resides within each and every one of us.

The Transformative Power of the Law of Abundance

The Law of Abundance is a universal principle that applies to all areas of life. It is the idea that there is an infinite supply of abundance and prosperity available to us if we are willing to align ourselves with it. By focusing our thoughts and energy on abundance, we can attract more of it into our lives. This can take many forms, such as financial abundance, success in our careers, fulfilling relationships, and a sense of purpose and meaning in life.

One of the most transformative aspects of the Law of Abundance is its ability to shift our mindset from one of scarcity to one of abundance. When we operate from a scarcity mindset, we tend to focus on what we lack and what we are afraid of losing. This can lead to feelings of anxiety, stress, and unhappiness. However, when we shift our mindset to one of abundance, we begin to focus on what we have and what we are grateful for. This can lead to feelings of joy, contentment, and fulfillment.

Encouragement for Continued Growth and Self Improvement

The journey toward abundance is a lifelong one. It requires a commitment to ongoing growth and self-improvement. As you continue on your journey, remember to be patient with yourself and celebrate your progress along the way. There will be times when you encounter obstacles and setbacks, but these are opportunities for growth and learning. By embracing these challenges and using them as opportunities to learn and grow, you will continue to move forward on your path toward abundance.

Remember that the Law of Abundance is not a one-time fix. It requires consistent effort and dedication to maintain a positive mindset and attract abundance into your life. This may involve daily practices such as meditation, visualization, affirmations, and gratitude exercises. It may also involve setting goals, taking action, and cultivating healthy habits.

The Limitless Potential of an Abundant Life

The Law of Abundance holds the key to unlocking your limitless potential. When you align yourself with abundance, you open yourself up to a world of opportunities and possibilities. You begin to see the world in a different light, with a sense of hope and optimism. You begin to believe in yourself and your ability to create the life you desire.

An abundant life is not just about financial wealth, although that can be an important part of it. It is about living a life that is rich in all areas, including relationships, health, personal growth, and spiritual fulfillment. It is about finding your purpose and living it fully. It is about being the best version of yourself and making a positive impact on the world around you.

In conclusion, the Law of Abundance is a powerful force that can transform your life in countless ways. By understanding and applying its principles, you can attract wealth, success, and fulfillment into your life. Remember to stay committed to ongoing growth and self-improvement, and to maintain a positive mindset as you continue on your journey toward abundance. The potential for an abundant life is limitless – it is up to you to unlock it.

THANK YOU

Thank You for Taking the Journey Towards Abundance

Congratulations! By reading this book and implementing the principles outlined in each chapter, you have taken a significant step towards transforming your life and embracing the Law of Abundance. Your commitment to personal growth and your willingness to apply the strategies shared here are essential components of your journey towards greater wealth and success.

As you continue to explore the concepts outlined in this book, remember that you are not alone on this journey. By sharing your experiences and insights with others, you can help create a community of like-minded individuals who are also committed to living an abundant life. Together, we can all achieve greater levels of success, wealth, and fulfillment, unlocking the limitless potential that resides within each and every one of us.

First and foremost, I want to express my sincere gratitude for your dedication to personal growth. The Law of Abundance is not a quick fix or a one-size-fits-all solution, but a lifelong journey towards achieving greater wealth and success. Your willingness to invest time and effort into your personal growth is a testament to your commitment to creating a life of abundance.

It's important to acknowledge that we are all on this journey towards abundance together. We are all interconnected, and our individual growth and success can have a ripple effect on the world around us. By working together and supporting each other, we can create a collective journey towards greater abundance for all.

I encourage you to share your experiences and insights with others. By sharing your journey towards abundance, you can inspire and motivate others to take action towards their own goals. Whether it's through social media, blogging, or simply talking to friends and family, your experiences and insights can make a significant impact on those around you.

Remember that every journey towards abundance is unique, and there is no one-size-fits-all solution. Share your successes and your challenges, and don't be afraid to ask for help when you need it. Together, we can support each other towards achieving greater levels of success and abundance.

Thank you for joining me on this incredible journey towards abundance. The Law of Abundance is a powerful tool for achieving greater wealth, success, and fulfillment in life. By implementing the strategies outlined in each chapter, you can create a personalized plan for attracting abundance into your life.

Remember that abundance is not just about money or material possessions, but about creating a life of purpose, meaning, and joy. By aligning your goals with your values and taking action towards your dreams, you can create a life of abundance that is fulfilling and meaningful.

Once again, thank you for your commitment to personal growth and your willingness to explore the Law of Abundance. I wish you all the best on your journey towards greater wealth, success, and fulfillment.

www.ingramcontent.com/pod-product-compliance
Lightning Source LLC
Chambersburg PA
CBHW070603220526
45467CB00003B/1280